JOURNAL

Self Coaching Models

C: Circumstance
T: Thought
F: Feeling
A: Actions
R: Result

Unintentional Model

C...

T...

F...

A...

A...

A...

R...

Intentional Model

C...

T...

F...

A...

A...

A...

R...

NOTES

....

....

....

....

....

....

....

Unintentional Model

C..

T..

F..

A..

A..

A..

R..

Intentional Model

C..

T..

F..

A..

A..

A..

R..

NOTES

....

....

....

....

....

....

....

Unintentional Model

C...

T...

F...

A...

A...

A...

R...

Intentional Model

C...

T...

F...

A...

A...

A...

R...

NOTES

....

....

....

....

....

....

....

Unintentional Model

C...

T...

F...

A...

A...

A...

R...

Intentional Model

C...

T...

F...

A...

A...

A...

R...

NOTES

....

....

....

....

....

....

....

Unintentional Model

C...

T...

F...

A...

A...

A...

R...

Intentional Model

C...

T...

F...

A...

A...

A...

R...

NOTES

....

....

....

....

....

....

....

Unintentional Model

C...

T...

F...

A...

A...

A...

R...

Intentional Model

C...

T...

F...

A...

A...

A...

R...

NOTES

....

....

....

....

....

....

....

Unintentional Model

C..

T..

F..

A..

A..

A..

R..

Intentional Model

C..

T..

F..

A..

A..

A..

R..

NOTES

....

....

....

....

....

....

....

Unintentional Model

C...

T...

F...

A...

A...

A...

R...

Intentional Model

C...

T...

F...

A...

A...

A...

R...

NOTES

....

....

....

....

....

....

....

Unintentional Model

C...

T...

F...

A...

A...

A...

R...

Intentional Model

C...

T...

F...

A...

A...

A...

R...

NOTES

....

....

....

....

....

....

....

Unintentional Model

C.......................................

T.......................................

F.......................................

A.......................................

A.......................................

A.......................................

R.......................................

Intentional Model

C.......................................

T.......................................

F.......................................

A.......................................

A.......................................

A.......................................

R.......................................

NOTES

....

....

....

....

....

....

....

Unintentional Model

C...

T...

F...

A...

A...

A...

R...

Intentional Model

C...

T...

F...

A...

A...

A...

R...

NOTES

....

....

....

....

....

....

....

Unintentional Model

C................................

T................................

F................................

A................................

A................................

A................................

R................................

Intentional Model

C................................

T................................

F................................

A................................

A................................

A................................

R................................

NOTES

....

....

....

....

....

....

....

Unintentional Model

C...

T...

F...

A...

A...

A...

R...

Intentional Model

C...

T...

F...

A...

A...

A...

R...

NOTES

....

....

....

....

....

....

....

Unintentional Model

C..

T..

F..

A..

A..

A..

R..

Intentional Model

C..

T..

F..

A..

A..

A..

R..

NOTES

....

....

....

....

....

....

....

Unintentional Model

C...

T...

F...

A...

A...

A...

R...

Intentional Model

C...

T...

F...

A...

A...

A...

R...

NOTES

....

....

....

....

....

....

....

Unintentional Model

C..

T..

F..

A..

A..

A..

R..

Intentional Model

C..

T..

F..

A..

A..

A..

R..

NOTES

....

....

....

....

....

....

....

Unintentional Model

C..............................

T..............................

F..............................

A..............................

A..............................

A..............................

R..............................

Intentional Model

C..............................

T..............................

F..............................

A..............................

A..............................

A..............................

R..............................

NOTES

....

....

....

....

....

....

....

Unintentional Model

C..

T..

F..

A..

A..

A..

R..

Intentional Model

C..

T..

F..

A..

A..

A..

R..

NOTES

....

....

....

....

....

....

....

Unintentional Model

C..

T..

F..

A..

A..

A..

R..

Intentional Model

C..

T..

F..

A..

A..

A..

R..

NOTES

....

....

....

....

....

....

....

Unintentional Model

C..

T..

F..

A..

A..

A..

R..

Intentional Model

C..

T..

F..

A..

A..

A..

R..

NOTES

....

....

....

....

....

....

....

Unintentional Model

C......................................

T......................................

F......................................

A......................................

A......................................

A......................................

R......................................

Intentional Model

C......................................

T......................................

F......................................

A......................................

A......................................

A......................................

R......................................

NOTES

....

....

....

....

....

....

....

Unintentional Model

C...

T...

F...

A...

A...

A...

R...

Intentional Model

C...

T...

F...

A...

A...

A...

R...

NOTES

....

....

....

....

....

....

....

Unintentional Model

C..

T..

F..

A..

A..

A..

R..

Intentional Model

C..

T..

F..

A..

A..

A..

R..

NOTES

....

....

....

....

....

....

....

Unintentional Model

C..

T..

F..

A..

A..

A..

R..

Intentional Model

C..

T..

F..

A..

A..

A..

R..

NOTES

....

....

....

....

....

....

....

Unintentional Model

C...

T...

F...

A...

A...

A...

R...

Intentional Model

C...

T...

F...

A...

A...

A...

R...

NOTES

....

....

....

....

....

....

....

Unintentional Model

C...

T...

F...

A...

A...

A...

R...

Intentional Model

C...

T...

F...

A...

A...

A...

R...

NOTES

....

....

....

....

....

....

....

Unintentional Model

C.......................................

T.......................................

F.......................................

A.......................................

A.......................................

A.......................................

R.......................................

Intentional Model

C.......................................

T.......................................

F.......................................

A.......................................

A.......................................

A.......................................

R.......................................

NOTES

....

....

....

....

....

....

....

Unintentional Model

C...

T...

F...

A...

A...

A...

R...

Intentional Model

C...

T...

F...

A...

A...

A...

R...

NOTES

....

....

....

....

....

....

....

Unintentional Model

C..

T..

F..

A..

A..

A..

R..

Intentional Model

C..

T..

F..

A..

A..

A..

R..

NOTES

....

....

....

....

....

....

....

Unintentional Model

C..

T..

F..

A..

A..

A..

R..

Intentional Model

C..

T..

F..

A..

A..

A..

R..

NOTES

....

....

....

....

....

....

....

Unintentional Model

C..................................

T..................................

F..................................

A..................................

A..................................

A..................................

R..................................

Intentional Model

C..................................

T..................................

F..................................

A..................................

A..................................

A..................................

R..................................

NOTES

....

....

....

....

....

....

....

Unintentional Model

C..

T..

F..

A..

A..

A..

R..

Intentional Model

C..

T..

F..

A..

A..

A..

R..

NOTES

....

....

....

....

....

....

....

Unintentional Model

C..

T..

F..

A..

A..

A..

R..

Intentional Model

C..

T..

F..

A..

A..

A..

R..

NOTES

....

....

....

....

....

....

....

Unintentional Model

C...

T...

F...

A...

A...

A...

R...

Intentional Model

C...

T...

F...

A...

A...

A...

R...

NOTES

....

....

....

....

....

....

....

Unintentional Model

C......................................

T......................................

F......................................

A......................................

A......................................

A......................................

R......................................

Intentional Model

C......................................

T......................................

F......................................

A......................................

A......................................

A......................................

R......................................

NOTES

....

....

....

....

....

....

....

Unintentional Model

C...

T...

F...

A...

A...

A...

R...

Intentional Model

C...

T...

F...

A...

A...

A...

R...

NOTES

....

....

....

....

....

....

....

Unintentional Model

C..................................

T..................................

F..................................

A..................................

A..................................

A..................................

R..................................

Intentional Model

C..................................

T..................................

F..................................

A..................................

A..................................

A..................................

R..................................

NOTES

....

....

....

....

....

....

....

Unintentional Model

C.......................................

T.......................................

F.......................................

A.......................................

A.......................................

A.......................................

R.......................................

Intentional Model

C.......................................

T.......................................

F.......................................

A.......................................

A.......................................

A.......................................

R.......................................

NOTES

....

....

....

....

....

....

....

Unintentional Model

C..

T..

F..

A..

A..

A..

R..

Intentional Model

C..

T..

F..

A..

A..

A..

R..

NOTES

....

....

....

....

....

....

....

Unintentional Model

C.......................................

T.......................................

F.......................................

A.......................................

A.......................................

A.......................................

R.......................................

Intentional Model

C.......................................

T.......................................

F.......................................

A.......................................

A.......................................

A.......................................

R.......................................

NOTES

....

....

....

....

....

....

....

Unintentional Model

C.................................

T.................................

F.................................

A.................................

A.................................

A.................................

R.................................

Intentional Model

C.................................

T.................................

F.................................

A.................................

A.................................

A.................................

R.................................

NOTES

....

....

....

....

....

....

....

Unintentional Model

C...

T...

F...

A...

A...

A...

R...

Intentional Model

C...

T...

F...

A...

A...

A...

R...

NOTES

....

....

....

....

....

....

....

Unintentional Model

C..

T..

F..

A..

A..

A..

R..

Intentional Model

C..

T..

F..

A..

A..

A..

R..

NOTES

....

....

....

....

....

....

....

Unintentional Model

C..

T..

F..

A..

A..

A..

R..

Intentional Model

C..

T..

F..

A..

A..

A..

R..

NOTES

....

....

....

....

....

....

....

Unintentional Model

C..

T..

F..

A..

A..

A..

R..

Intentional Model

C..

T..

F..

A..

A..

A..

R..

NOTES

....

....

....

....

....

....

....

Unintentional Model

C...

T...

F...

A...

A...

A...

R...

Intentional Model

C...

T...

F...

A...

A...

A...

R...

NOTES

....

....

....

....

....

....

....

Unintentional Model

C.......................................

T.......................................

F.......................................

A.......................................

A.......................................

A.......................................

R.......................................

Intentional Model

C.......................................

T.......................................

F.......................................

A.......................................

A.......................................

A.......................................

R.......................................

NOTES

....

....

....

....

....

....

....

Unintentional Model

C...

T...

F...

A...

A...

A...

R...

Intentional Model

C...

T...

F...

A...

A...

A...

R...

NOTES

....

....

....

....

....

....

....

Unintentional Model

C...

T...

F...

A...

A...

A...

R...

Intentional Model

C...

T...

F...

A...

A...

A...

R...

NOTES

....

....

....

....

....

....

....

Unintentional Model

C...

T...

F...

A...

A...

A...

R...

Intentional Model

C...

T...

F...

A...

A...

A...

R...

NOTES

....

....

....

....

....

....

....

Unintentional Model

C..

T..

F..

A..

A..

A..

R..

Intentional Model

C..

T..

F..

A..

A..

A..

R..

NOTES

....

....

....

....

....

....

....

Unintentional Model

C..

T..

F..

A..

A..

A..

R..

Intentional Model

C..

T..

F..

A..

A..

A..

R..

NOTES

....

....

....

....

....

....

....

Unintentional Model

C...

T...

F...

A...

A...

A...

R...

Intentional Model

C...

T...

F...

A...

A...

A...

R...

NOTES

....

....

....

....

....

....

....

Unintentional Model

C...

T...

F...

A...

A...

A...

R...

Intentional Model

C...

T...

F...

A...

A...

A...

R...

NOTES

....

....

....

....

....

....

....

Unintentional Model

C......................................

T......................................

F......................................

A......................................

A......................................

A......................................

R......................................

Intentional Model

C......................................

T......................................

F......................................

A......................................

A......................................

A......................................

R......................................

NOTES

....

....

....

....

....

....

....

Unintentional Model

C...

T...

F...

A...

A...

A...

R...

Intentional Model

C...

T...

F...

A...

A...

A...

R...

NOTES

....

....

....

....

....

....

....

Unintentional Model

C...

T...

F...

A...

A...

A...

R...

Intentional Model

C...

T...

F...

A...

A...

A...

R...

NOTES

....

....

....

....

....

....

....

Unintentional Model

C...

T...

F...

A...

A...

A...

R...

Intentional Model

C...

T...

F...

A...

A...

A...

R...

NOTES

....

....

....

....

....

....

....

Unintentional Model

C..

T..

F..

A..

A..

A..

R..

Intentional Model

C..

T..

F..

A..

A..

A..

R..

NOTES

....

....

....

....

....

....

....

Unintentional Model

C...

T...

F...

A...

A...

A...

R...

Intentional Model

C...

T...

F...

A...

A...

A...

R...

NOTES

....

....

....

....

....

....

....

Unintentional Model

C.....................................

T.....................................

F.....................................

A....................................

A.....................................

A......................................

R......................................

Intentional Model

C....................................

T....................................

F.....................................

A....................................

A....................................

A.....................................

R....................................

NOTES

....

....

....

....

....

....

....

Unintentional Model

C...

T...

F...

A...

A...

A...

R...

Intentional Model

C...

T...

F...

A...

A...

A...

R...

NOTES

....

....

....

....

....

....

....

Unintentional Model

C...

T...

F...

A...

A...

A...

R...

Intentional Model

C...

T...

F...

A...

A...

A...

R...

NOTES

....

....

....

....

....

....

....

Unintentional Model

C..

T..

F..

A..

A..

A..

R..

Intentional Model

C..

T..

F..

A..

A..

A..

R..

NOTES

....

....

....

....

....

....

....

Unintentional Model

C....................................

T....................................

F....................................

A....................................

A....................................

A....................................

R....................................

Intentional Model

C....................................

T....................................

F....................................

A....................................

A....................................

A....................................

R....................................

NOTES

....

....

....

....

....

....

....

Unintentional Model

C...

T...

F...

A...

A...

A...

R...

Intentional Model

C...

T...

F...

A...

A...

A...

R...

NOTES

....

....

....

....

....

....

....

Unintentional Model

C...

T...

F...

A...

A...

A...

R...

Intentional Model

C...

T...

F...

A...

A...

A...

R...

NOTES

....

....

....

....

....

....

....

Unintentional Model

C..

T..

F..

A..

A..

A..

R..

Intentional Model

C..

T..

F..

A..

A..

A..

R..

NOTES

....

....

....

....

....

....

....

Unintentional Model

C..

T..

F..

A..

A..

A..

R..

Intentional Model

C..

T..

F..

A..

A..

A..

R..

NOTES

....

....

....

....

....

....

....

Unintentional Model

C...

T...

F...

A...

A...

A...

R...

Intentional Model

C...

T...

F...

A...

A...

A...

R...

NOTES

....

....

....

....

....

....

....

Unintentional Model

C....................................

T....................................

F....................................

A....................................

A....................................

A....................................

R....................................

Intentional Model

C....................................

T....................................

F....................................

A....................................

A....................................

A....................................

R....................................

NOTES

....

....

....

....

....

....

....

Unintentional Model

C..

T..

F..

A..

A..

A..

R..

Intentional Model

C..

T..

F..

A..

A..

A..

R..

NOTES

....

....

....

....

....

....

....

Unintentional Model

C...

T...

F...

A...

A...

A...

R...

Intentional Model

C...

T...

F...

A...

A...

A...

R...

NOTES

....

....

....

....

....

....

....

Unintentional Model

C..

T..

F..

A..

A..

A..

R..

Intentional Model

C..

T..

F..

A..

A..

A..

R..

NOTES

....

....

....

....

....

....

....

Unintentional Model

C..

T..

F..

A..

A..

A..

R..

Intentional Model

C..

T..

F..

A..

A..

A..

R..

NOTES

....

....

....

....

....

....

....

Unintentional Model

C...

T...

F...

A...

A...

A...

R...

Intentional Model

C...

T...

F...

A...

A...

A...

R...

NOTES

....

....

....

....

....

....

....

Unintentional Model

C..

T..

F..

A..

A..

A..

R..

Intentional Model

C..

T..

F..

A..

A..

A..

R..

NOTES

....

....

....

....

....

....

....

Unintentional Model

C..

T..

F..

A..

A..

A..

R..

Intentional Model

C..

T..

F..

A..

A..

A..

R..

NOTES

....

....

....

....

....

....

....

Unintentional Model

C...

T...

F...

A...

A...

A...

R...

Intentional Model

C...

T...

F...

A...

A...

A...

R...

NOTES

....

....

....

....

....

....

....

Unintentional Model

C......................................

T......................................

F......................................

A......................................

A......................................

A......................................

R......................................

Intentional Model

C......................................

T......................................

F......................................

A......................................

A......................................

A......................................

R......................................

NOTES

....

....

....

....

....

....

....

Unintentional Model

C..

T..

F..

A..

A..

A..

R..

Intentional Model

C..

T..

F..

A..

A..

A..

R..

NOTES

....

....

....

....

....

....

....

Unintentional Model

C.......................................

T.......................................

F.......................................

A.......................................

A.......................................

A.......................................

R.......................................

Intentional Model

C.......................................

T.......................................

F.......................................

A.......................................

A.......................................

A.......................................

R.......................................

NOTES

....

....

....

....

....

....

....

Unintentional Model

C......................................

T......................................

F......................................

A......................................

A......................................

A......................................

R......................................

Intentional Model

C......................................

T......................................

F......................................

A......................................

A......................................

A......................................

R......................................

NOTES

....

....

....

....

....

....

....

Unintentional Model

C...

T...

F...

A...

A...

A...

R...

Intentional Model

C...

T...

F...

A...

A...

A...

R...

NOTES

....

....

....

....

....

....

....

Unintentional Model

C..

T..

F..

A..

A..

A..

R..

Intentional Model

C..

T..

F..

A..

A..

A..

R..

NOTES

....

....

....

....

....

....

....

Unintentional Model

C..

T..

F..

A..

A..

A..

R..

Intentional Model

C..

T..

F..

A..

A..

A..

R..

NOTES

....

....

....

....

....

....

....

Unintentional Model

C..

T..

F..

A..

A..

A..

R..

Intentional Model

C..

T..

F..

A..

A..

A..

R..

NOTES

....

....

....

....

....

....

....

Unintentional Model

C...

T...

F...

A...

A...

A...

R...

Intentional Model

C...

T...

F...

A...

A...

A...

R...

NOTES

....

....

....

....

....

....

....

Unintentional Model

C...

T...

F...

A...

A...

A...

R...

Intentional Model

C...

T...

F...

A...

A...

A...

R...

NOTES

....

....

....

....

....

....

....

Unintentional Model

C...

T...

F...

A...

A...

A...

R...

Intentional Model

C...

T...

F...

A...

A...

A...

R...

NOTES

....

....

....

....

....

....

....

Unintentional Model

C..

T..

F..

A..

A..

A..

R..

Intentional Model

C..

T..

F..

A..

A..

A..

R..

NOTES

....

....

....

....

....

....

....

Unintentional Model

C...

T...

F...

A...

A...

A...

R...

Intentional Model

C...

T...

F...

A...

A...

A...

R...

NOTES

....

....

....

....

....

....

....

Unintentional Model

C..

T..

F..

A..

A..

A..

R..

Intentional Model

C..

T..

F..

A..

A..

A..

R..

NOTES

....

....

....

....

....

....

....

Unintentional Model

C..

T..

F..

A..

A..

A..

R..

Intentional Model

C..

T..

F..

A..

A..

A..

R..

NOTES

....

....

....

....

....

....

....

Unintentional Model

C...

T...

F...

A...

A...

A...

R...

Intentional Model

C...

T...

F...

A...

A...

A...

R...

NOTES

....

....

....

....

....

....

....

Unintentional Model

C...

T...

F...

A...

A...

A...

R...

Intentional Model

C...

T...

F...

A...

A...

A...

R...

NOTES

....

....

....

....

....

....

....

Unintentional Model

C..

T..

F..

A..

A..

A..

R..

Intentional Model

C..

T..

F..

A..

A..

A..

R..

NOTES

....

....

....

....

....

....

....

Unintentional Model

C...

T...

F...

A...

A...

A...

R...

Intentional Model

C...

T...

F...

A...

A...

A...

R...

NOTES

....

....

....

....

....

....

....

Unintentional Model

C..

T..

F..

A..

A..

A..

R..

Intentional Model

C..

T..

F..

A..

A..

A..

R..

NOTES

....

....

....

....

....

....

....

Unintentional Model

C...

T...

F...

A...

A...

A...

R...

Intentional Model

C...

T...

F...

A...

A...

A...

R...

NOTES

....

....

....

....

....

....

....